REBECCA MORDAN

After graduating from Sheffield University and Bristol Old Vic Theatre School, Rebecca worked as an actor, director, MC, writer and producer, was a regular commentator on TV and radio, including many years as a 'rent-a-feminist' on Sky News. In 2002, she founded award-winning feminist production hub Scary Little Girls, opening in London with *Dracula: The Kisses* which centred a female Count Dracula. With SLG and comedian and blogger Jennifer Kennedy, she hosts South West sell-out hit *Queenagers*, a cabaret about menopause set to tour the UK and abroad in 2026/7.

In 2018, Rebecca founded the *Greenham Women Everywhere* project which has interviewed over 200 Greenham Women; she is now working with writer and director Rachel Tunnard on a feature film for BBC about Greenham Common Women's Peace Camp and is featured in documentaries on the subject including *Gentle Angry Women* (Folkfilms), and *Women Against the Bomb* (ARTE Films).

In 2021 she was a member of the BBC Writersroom, wrote *The Greenham Effect* for the BBC's Archive on Four, *Camborne* for Radio 4's The UK Project and her first book was published by The History Press: *Out of the Darkness: Greenham Voices 1981-2000*.

Her second book, also with The History Press, titled *No Woman is an Island,* based on her work interviewing women living on the remote Isles of Scilly, is coming out in Spring 2027.

www.scarylittlegirls.co.uk

First published in the UK in 2026 by Aurora Metro Publications Ltd.

80 Hill Rise, Richmond, TW10 6UB. Published in association with Historic Royal Palaces www.hrp.org.uk

www.aurorametro.com   info@aurorametro.com

X:@aurorametro FB: /AuroraMetroBooks

Sophia Duleep Singh: Princess, Suffragette, Trailblazer by Rebecca Mordan © Historic Royal Palaces 2026

Cover Illustration by Kushiaania

Cover design copyright Aurora Metro Books © 2026

Editing & Production: Cheryl Robson

Printed in the UK by 4edge Ltd, Essex on sustainably resourced paper.

ISBNs: 978-1-910798-11-9 (print)

978-1-910798-12-6 (ebook)

SOPHIA DULEEP SINGH

PRINCESS, SUFFRAGETTE, TRAILBLAZER

BY

REBECCA MORDAN

AURORA METRO BOOKS

Sophia Duleep Singh in 1930. Photo: © Peter Bance

Preface

When Rebecca Mordan founded Scary Little Girls in 2002, it was to celebrate unsung, misunderstood or overlooked heroines; to rescue them, as feminist satirist Jacky Fleming says, 'from the dustbin of history'. Imagine, then, our excitement and honour when we were approached by Historic Royal Palaces to develop a theatre performance with them centred on the life of Princess Sophia Duleep Singh, daughter of the last Maharaja of the Punjab, goddaughter of Queen Victoria, and selfless activist for the rights of others.

As the play developed, it took on the characteristics of the woman at its centre. Specifically created for school audiences and students aged 11-14, we knew it had to be fast-paced, interactive and informative, like the suffrage campaigns Sophia undertook; we wanted it to be fun, big hearted and empowering, as those that knew Sophia tell us she was; and we created it to galvanise and inspire, so that those who saw it and also saw injustice in their own lives could gain confidence from Sophia's extraordinary story and know that another world is both positive and possible!

The result is this 50-minute whistle-stop tour of Sophia's life, actions and beliefs, her loves and losses, depressions and triumphs, which has been performed to over 30,000 students across the UK since 2023. It covers themes of gender, racial and sexual equality and encourages discussions about identity, empire, family and language. It shows the difference we can make for each other and the world, while also enhancing and enriching our own experiences.

We are hugely grateful to the team at Historic Royal Palaces who gave us access to this astonishing story, helped develop it into the play you hold in your hands and support it going out on the road twice a year to reach students from all backgrounds. Thank you to the women who wrote about Sophia before us, in particular Anita Anand; to all the students and teachers who have welcomed us into their schools, and to the wonderful actors that have brought the show to life. As Sophia's tale demonstrates, we are stronger together and together we persist.

– Rebecca Mordan (writer)
& Vanessa Pini (director)
Scary Little Girls

The Indian Princess Who Fought For Women's Rights

Princess Sophia Duleep Singh (1876–1948) is best known as a suffragette, the daughter of deposed Maharajah Duleep Singh and goddaughter of Queen Victoria (1837–1901).

Born on 8 August 1876, Sophia was the granddaughter of Ranjit Singh, the Maharajah of the Punjab in the north-west of the Indian Subcontinent. After the death of Ranjit Singh and the assassination of three of his successors, Sophia's father, Duleep Singh (then aged 5), became Maharajah, with his mother Jind Kaur acting as regent of the Sikh Empire on his behalf. Following her armies' defeat in the Anglo-Sikh Wars, their kingdom in Punjab was lost, and Jind was imprisoned, forcibly separated from her child for thirteen years when he was sent to England in 1854.

Duleep Singh (1838–93) married Bamba Müller (1848–87), the daughter of a German banker and enslaved Ethiopian woman, in 1864. They had seven children, of which Sophia was second youngest. In England, he met Queen Victoria who was captivated by the young Maharajah, and they formed a lasting and genuine, if fundamentally unequal, relationship. The Queen later became godmother to two of Duleep Singh's children, including Princess Sophia.

Sophia Duleep Singh as a baby with her mother, Maharani Bamba.
Photo: © Peter Bance

Elveden Hall

Sophia's early childhood was spent at Elveden Hall in Suffolk, which her father purchased in 1863 for his growing family. Here, the children enjoyed an indulged childhood with exotic pets, toys and fancy-dress parties. However, by 1886, the fortunes of the family had declined, mainly because of Duleep Singh's lavish lifestyle and the running costs of Elveden Hall, exacerbated by the India Office failing to fully recompense him for his seized wealth in Lahore. The grand house had to be sold. In desperation, Sophia's father took his family and attempted to return to India to claim what he was owed. They got as far as Yemen before he was arrested. Determined, he eventually put his wife and children on a ship back to England and stayed to continue his campaign. He never returned to his family.

The Death of Bamba Müller

Maharani Bamba and the children were effectively homeless and penniless. Bamba struggled to cope with her husband's abandonment, overcome by grief and despair. The India Office intervened at Queen Victoria's request, finding Bamba and the children a home in London. In 1887, Sophia contracted typhoid fever. Her desperate mother refused to leave her bedside, even as her own health deteriorated. On 16 September, Maharani Bamba was found dead next to her sleeping daughter, having collapsed and slipped into a coma.

After the death of their mother, Arthur Oliphant, an Indian Political Service official, was appointed to look after the younger members of the family who moved into the Oliphant family home in Brighton.

Princess Sophia with her horse and dogs. Photo: © Peter Bance

Princess Sophia at Hampton Court Palace

In 1896, Queen Victoria granted Princess Sophia the use of Faraday House, then part of the Hampton Court estate, as a grace-and-favour residence plus £200 a year to maintain it. Like her sisters, Sophia inherited the sizeable sum of £23,000 from her father when he died in 1893, which meant that she was independently wealthy and able to pursue her own interests.

Sophia had a real zest for life and many passions. She was sporty, playing hockey and riding and cycling frequently. She was a keen animal lover and kept parrots and tortoises at Faraday House but her real love was dogs, and she became a leading breeder and trainer. She especially loved Pomeranians and Borzoi hounds and was often seen walking her dogs around the grounds of Hampton Court Palace, including through the famous Maze! Her other hobbies included photography and music, and she kept a wide range of instruments in her home.

Hampton Court Palace in the early 20th century. Sophia regularly walked her dogs in the palace grounds while she lived at Faraday House.
Photo: © Historic Royal Palaces

Sophia the Suffragette

Through her connections, Sophia became aware of the women's suffrage movement and used her wealth and status to further the cause. She was an active member of the Women's Social Political Union (WSPU) and was often seen selling *The Suffragette* newspaper at her pitch outside Hampton Court Palace, an activity that even the King tried to intervene in.

From her home at Hampton Court, Sophia participated in the mass boycott of the 1911 census. Along with others who could afford to risk the fine, she spoiled the census form sent to record the whereabouts of every citizen in the country – on the basis that if women were not allowed the vote, they refused to be counted as citizens.

Sophia selling subscriptions to the Suffragette newspaper on her pitch outside Hampton Court Palace in 1913. Photo: © Museum of London

No Vote, No Tax!

Sophia was also a leading member of the Women's Tax Resistance League (WTRL), which campaigned on the principle 'No vote, No tax!'. She was arrested for her activism and appeared in court three times for refusing to pay taxes. She declared: 'When the women of England are enfranchised and the state acknowledges me as a citizen I shall, of course, pay my share willingly towards its upkeep.'

In 1918, the Representation of the People Act granted the vote to some women over 30 in Britain. This was a significant step towards equality, but it would be another 10 years before women were finally given the vote on the same terms as men. Even after women won the vote, this was not the end of the matter for Princess Sophia who continued to campaign for equality all her life.

A Friend to Many

Sophia's philanthropy extended far beyond women's rights, and she supported many individuals and causes, particularly those affecting Indians. She formed close ties with the Sikh community in London, visiting the Sikh Temple at Shepherd's Bush regularly. When the First World War broke out in 1914, the WSPU and WTRL temporarily ceased activity and Princess Sophia used her time and celebrity to support the war effort. In 1915, she was part of the 10,000-strong Women's War Work Procession led by Emmeline Pankhurst and joined the Voluntary Auxiliary Detachment Service as a nurse, working at Isleworth Hospital for two years. She also promoted the plight of Indian seamen and sailors – known as Lascars – stranded in London, raising enough money to help build a safe haven called the Lascars Club.

Left to right Princesses Bamba, Catherine and Sophia Duleep Singh at their debut at Buckingham Palace in May 1895. Photo: © Peter Bance

During the Second World War, Sophia moved to Buckinghamshire to be close to her sister Catherine (see below) where they took in young evacuees from west London. Siblings John, Michael and Shirley Sarbutt remembered the stay fondly, recalling oriental ornaments, ample food and a parrot called Akbar. During air raids they would squeeze into the air raid shelter surrounded by the princesses' dogs.

Death and Legacy

Princess Sophia Duleep Singh died in her sleep on 22 August 1948. On her instructions, a full band played Wagner's 'Funeral March' at her cremation. Her ashes were taken to India for burial.

Although not a fan of public speaking, and often anxious not to draw attention away from fellow suffragettes, Sophia's celebrity was ultimately an important asset for the suffragette movement. She dedicated her life to the fight for equality and the support of others. In the 1934 edition of *The Women's Who's Who*, which recorded careers of leading women of the era, Sophia listed 'Advancement of Women' as her only interest.

Catherine and Bamba

Sophia's two sisters, Catherine and Bamba also feature in this play. Like Sophia, Princess Catherine Duleep Singh (1871–1941) dedicated her life to the fight for equality and the support of others. She campaigned peacefully for votes for women, supporting the National Union of Women's Suffrage Societies (NUWSS), joining committees, attending events and giving financial assistance. Catherine spent much of her life in Germany with her partner, Lina Schäfer. The pair were devoted to each other, and their time together profoundly impacted Catherine's life. Before her return to England on Lina's death, Catherine acted as a guarantor for four Jewish families, enabling them to escape Nazi Germany for England. She opened her house in Buckinghamshire to the refugees, some of whom lived with her until her death in 1941.

Princess Bamba (1859–1957), the oldest of Sophia's sisters, considered herself heir to her grandfather Ranjit Singh's empire, and returned to live in Lahore in the 1940s where she agitated for the return of her family's stolen lands – without success.

She generously supported many charities, especially girls' schools, forged friendships with prominent local South Asians and made connections with several members of the Indian liberation movement.

Acknowledgements

This play would not have been possible without the dedication and creativity of several key individuals and teams.

We would like to thank Rebecca Mordan and Vanessa Pini at Scary Little Girls who wrote, and continue to direct, this wonderful play.

The Schools team at Historic Royal Palaces brought their expertise and passion for storytelling to the project, which ensured that the play was grounded in history while remaining accessible and engaging for new generations.

Most importantly, we acknowledge Princess Sophia Duleep Singh and her fellow Suffragettes. We are forever indebted to their tireless work, personal sacrifices and relentless pursuit of equality. We hope this play serves as a fitting tribute to their courage and a reminder of the power of standing up for what is right.

SOPHIA DULEEP SINGH:

Princess, Suffragette, Trailblazer

REBECCA MORDAN

Actors play the following characters:
SOPHIA
JINDAN
BOSIE
BAMBA
CATHERINE
MAID
THE MADMAN
EMMELINE PANKHURST
ANNIE KENNEY
POLICEMAN
ASQUITH
JUDGE
CASTELLO
SISTER POWELL-SINCLAIR
EKAM
GUNEET

Note: In the original production, three actors doubled to play the roles.

The stage is set, the projector is ready and the lights are on.

The seating layout includes aisles that serve as acting areas, allowing the cast to perform amongst the audience. The cast should look for times to take the story into the audience as much as possible.

While the audience enter, a series of photographs are projected; three different sets on three different topics that run from the 1800s to the present day in a loop. The first set go from the suffrage campaign, including Black Friday and images of police violence to women; to the police man-handling women at the Sarah Everard protests in 2021. The second set from early images of the British colonisation of India, including scenes of glorious pageants from Britain establishing their hold on India early in their empire; famine and unrest as British reign takes hold, protests led by Gandhi, and go up to the Black Lives Matter protests and statue tipping of 2020. The third set covers the lascars, the cotton and indigo farmers exploitation and the present-day cost of 'cheap' textiles.

Once the audience is in and seated and any other announcements have been made by the school, the actor playing SOPHIA walks out to address the students. This needs to be delivered in the actor's own words, a way of bonding with the audience as much as informing them. The following content is what needs to be covered but the actor and director are free to work this opening section up in the rehearsal room so that it is right for the actor and sounds genuine. It should be about two minutes long max.

SOPHIA ACTOR Hello *(in as many languages as the actor knows).* We are here to perform a play about Sophia Duleep Singh that will be a little under an hour long. I'm one of the actors, the one playing Sophia actually. Sophia was Queen Victoria's goddaughter and later a suffragette and a campaigner for the rights of women, oppressed people and animals. This story is going to be told by me as Sophia and two other actors playing Sophia's grandmother and housekeeper. You're going to meet Sophia's sisters Catherine and Bamba and lots of other people she meets in her life. There's only three of us so sometimes the other two actors are going to play different roles, putting on bits of costume and different voices, you know, actor stuff. Right, I'm going to go and wait over here now because I'll be coming out again soon as Sophia, I'll see you in a bit!

The lights come up as a hunched female figure wrapped in dirty rags that trail behind her shuffles around and through the audience. As she moves towards the stage, she convinces an audience member to get hold of the edge of her rags, unfolding herself from them. There is a lot of them, and some are covered in writing in Indian languages. As she hurries the audience along and herself to the stage, she talks to those around her in Punjabi, complaining about the weather, how long it's taken her to get here, noting things she's interested in in the room or that audience members are wearing.

By the time she is on stage, JINDAN is revealed from underneath the rag cloth, not an aged beggar but a proud woman in the prime of her life in a clean white sari.

She speaks her first address to the audience dynamically, wasting no time, repeating some sections in rapid, crisp Urdu:

JINDAN Learned and esteemed friends, I am Jindan! At 18 I became wife to the Lion of Punjab, he who united the glorious peoples of India – the Hindus, the Muslims, the Sikhs! At 23 I was regent, ruling India for my infant son Duleep Singh, the last Maharajah, who I watched the British swindle and destroy. And today I have escaped the fetters of time to bring you the tale of my granddaughter, Sophia Duleep Singh – princess, suffragette, rebel!

While this is happening, from somewhere else in the room, BOSIE has entered, a sturdy, no nonsense sort of English housekeeper, dressed sensibly in a 1920s style overcoat and shoes, and through this speech she has been making her way to the stage by gathering in the cloth that JINDAN has spread over the audience.

BOSIE *(as she makes her way through the audience folding up the cloth)* Dear me, what a mess. If you can just hand me that, thanking you. Goodness, it needs a wash, don't it?

JINDAN *(trying to continue her narration)* Sophia, born in exile –

It is becoming increasingly hard to maintain the dignity and drama JINDAN was enjoying as BOSIE fusses over the cloth and chats with the audience. As so often with the exchanges between JINDAN and BOSIE throughout the play, these lines come hard on the heels of each other, often over-lapping or cutting in over each other.

BOSIE *(still making her way through the audience)* Don't mind me, I'm part of the story, I just never could bear to see a room a mess. *(to an audience member)* Do you know what I mean?

JINDAN Bosie! I'm trying to regale them with Sophia's royal Indian dynasty!

BOSIE *(taking a seat at the front and getting the audience to move over so she can fit)* Oh it was my life's dream to go to India! *(to audience)* If I can just squeeze in here, that's right, budge up a bit, thanking you. *(once seated, to all and JINDAN)* I wanted to see a real Indian Elephant!

JINDAN *(in Urdu)* My son saw his uncle pulled from an elephant and killed – (Haati! Meri beter neh aapenee chaché nu haati tum kichkey maaria dehkia!)

BOSIE Can we have the story in English, please?

JINDAN *(in English)* I'm using more than one language because Sophia's life was not simply one heritage. *(to the audience)* Who here can speak other languages, perhaps at home or with family?

JINDAN here does a little check in with the audience about what languages they speak. Once she has established that there are several more than just English in the room, she turns to BOSIE with a satisfied:

JINDAN You see?

BOSIE *(joining her on stage)* Well some of us aren't royalty getting fancy educations and learning lots of languages, we're just housekeepers – that's how I knew Sophia, I worked for her for donkey's years, bless her heart.

JINDAN My father was the stable man at the palace! My earliest memories are the breath of horses and cobbles covered in straw and manure under my bare feet!

BOSIE Alright, don't get het up, it's all in the past now, you are dead you know!

JINDAN So are you!

BOSIE You've been dead longer!

JINDAN Bosie, everyone in this story is dead.

BOSIE Then why are we talking about them?

JINDAN Because a story about Sophia is a story about change, and to know what we want to change we must examine everything. You knew Sophia, you must have seen how much it meant to her when she changed things for herself and others?

BOSIE And I saw the depression when she felt defeated by trying and failing!

JINDAN That indeed is the rub. All life is risk. But while you can't be sure you **can** change things, you can be sure that, if you do nothing, things will stay the same.

BOSIE *(considering her point, still not decided)* Gimmie an example of something you changed?

JINDAN Well, when my beloved husband died, it was custom in India that a truly devoted wife would follow her spouse into the flames of the pyre while his body was burned.

Jindan stands centre-stage and flames are projected on to her.

BOSIE It never was?!

JINDAN Yes, and I was very young, the Lion's most recent wife –

BOSIE How many did he have?

JINDAN He had 20 wives and many concubines –

BOSIE He never did! Those prickly things like big hedgehogs?

JINDAN Not porcupines, Bosie, concubines. They are ... like girlfriends. And four wives and seven concubines burnt themselves alive on my husband's pyre. But I refused! *(Projection snaps off)* I told the court I had more duty to my only son than to my dead husband.

BOSIE Good for you! A woman can't get anything useful done burnt to a crisp on a pyre! I can see where Sophia got her rebellious spark now!

JINDAN If the deceitful British hadn't stolen Punjab from her father Sophia might have –

BOSIE Now hang about! We British took Sophia's family in and then gave her a home at Hampton Court Palace no less! Queen Victoria herself loved her, made her her goddaughter!

JINDAN Ha! The same Queen Victoria whose government ordered me to be torn from my son's side and imprisoned when he was only 9? Then caused division and bloodshed across our kingdom setting Sikh against Hindu, Hindu against Muslim? *(she looks into the audience, asking them)* How old is this group? *(They answer)* My son was only 11 when he stood alone, and the British vultures made him sign away his own country forever!

BOSIE *(excited to join back in, overlapping the end of JINDAN's line)* They had vultures!

JINDAN *(confused by this seeming non sequitur)* What? Who?

BOSIE Sophia's family when she was growing up! Queen Victoria gave them a posh big house and Sophia's dad had all these foreign animals brought over and let them loose in the gardens.

JINDAN And yet, amidst the chaos, Sophia was a quiet, placid child, much loved by her older and younger siblings alike. Here she is look, trying to find her little brother Edward's favourite soldier to take with him to his first term at boarding school.

JINDAN reveals SOPHIA sat going through a toy chest.

SOPHIA *(going through the soldiers)* Here's generals Victor and Frederick and Ranjit and Nanak, though of course he doesn't fight, but where's Tiny Captain Edward?

BOSIE Dear little thing, her big sisters Catherine and Bamba should help her.

JINDAN Yes, they should.

BOSIE No, I mean, we should be her big sisters and help her, for this next bit of the story.

JINDAN Oh yes, of course. I'll be Bamba and you be Catherine.

BOSIE Righty-ho. Who's the oldest?

JINDAN Bamba, so I am.

BOSIE Ha!

JINDAN adds a blouse over her sari and BOSIE bustles out of her housecoat revealing a blouse the same colour as Jindan's, over a white shift suggesting an Edwardian style dress.

During this change, SOPHIA holds up a sign that says, 'Sophia's Nursery, the family home, Suffolk, 1886'.

SOPHIA *(reads the sign out loud and adds)* I'm 10!

BOSIE Are you ready?

JINDAN Yes, I'm Bamba now! *(indicates costume change to audience)*

BOSIE *(indicating her costume change also)* And I'm Catherine!

Immediately, solid BOSIE is transformed into a light young Princess in her late teens, CATHERINE, who goes up to SOPHIA with her coat folded up, as if helping SOPHIA to pack for their brother.

CATHERINE Here you go, Saff, Edward's winter coat, add this to his packing!

BAMBA I don't know why you two are making such a fuss, he's only going to school like Vic and Freddie did before him, and it didn't make them any worse, mind you they were boys to begin with so fairly beastly.

CATHERINE I think it's nice that Asa –

BAMBA Ah ah ah, only I can call her that!

CATHERINE – that Sophie takes care of her little brother.

SOPHIA Why do you say Victor and Freddie are beastly?

BAMBA Oh, Freddie's alright, he doesn't have that disappointed air the way Vic does when he sees one, always on at me to put up my hair or wear a corset! Of course, I shan't do either!

CATHERINE It's what husbands expect if you want to attract one.

BAMBA Don't think I do; brothers are bother enough.

CATHERINE I think you might be right, about the husband bit at least ...

SOPHIA Oh, I remember where I put Tiny Captain Eddie, he's in the field hospital! *(she goes to a bit of the stage and lifts some white cloth that has been used as a sheet for the several 'sick' toys underneath)* He had another one of his colds, you know.

SOPHIA picks the toy soldier up very tenderly and looks down at him with great concern. The two older sisters exchange a glance.

CATHERINE I think Eddie will be fine with his coat, Saff, he's getting those colds less than he did.

BAMBA It's this filthy climate, if the wretched British would let us go back to India, he'd probably be fine.

SOPHIA I don't want to live in India; I want to live here with you all like always!

BAMBA Well, I'm going to India just as soon as I can get out from under the peeping British noses, spying little coves! Saris not corsets!

SOPHIA *(to CATHERINE)* And you are going to Germany with your governess!

CATHERINE Only for a tour, I'll be back, and you'll never winkle Victor and Freddie out of England, they are quite the proper gentlemen.

BAMBA Oh yes, they fit right in, proper little *brown* English gentlemen!

SOPHIA What's wrong with that? *(Beat)* At least you can all write to me; Eddie and I are practising already so he's in the habit before he gets to school.

BAMBA Oh Sophie, he'll be busy when he gets to school!

SOPHIA He'll remember!

CATHERINE Of course he will. But then of course he's going to die.

SOPHIA He's going to what?!

CATHERINE/BOSIE Sorry, I didn't mean to say that as Catherine!

BAMBA/JINDAN *(as JINDAN to BOSIE, bundling her away from the scene with her coat)* Shut up, you ulu! *(as BAMBA reassuring her little sister)* She said the time will **fly** and we'll be back together before you know it, little Asa!

JINDAN joins BOSIE, leaving SOPHIA at the back centre of the stage writing letters, sitting on the floor piling up her correspondence to and from her different siblings.

BOSIE *(fully in narrator role again)* Well time does move on but only moves those Sophia loves further away.

BOSIE picks up a big stack of letters from SOPHIA who does not notice the narrators and carries on writing and organising her letters.

SOPHIA *(as she writes and adds to her piles)* Two Bamba, three Catherine.

BOSIE *(continued)* Letters become the life blood connecting the siblings across land and sea.

SOPHIA And I must get back to Eddie; he's sent me letters to pass on to our sisters.

JINDAN And some travel permanently beyond the reach of Sophia's letters or love. Her mother, weakened by years of alcohol abuse, collapses, slips into a coma and dies on Sophia's bedroom floor while watching over her daughter.

BOSIE She was driven to drink she was by Sophia's father! Spending all their money on parties and girlfriends, and then outright abandoning them in poverty!

Giving JINDAN half the letters.

SOPHIA is still writing but falling lower and lower over her papers ...

JINDAN My son should have been the Maharajah of mighty Indian kingdoms, not a caged prize for Britain's

Queen to pet and exhibit! Of course, so noble a nature strained at his fetters!

BOSIE *(talking to the audience)* Mothers and sons, eh? He went completely off the rails, gambled what money the British had promised him away and hot-footed it to Paris with his very age-inappropriate girlfriend! So, Sophia was alone for the death of her mother, and then her beloved Edward –

JINDAN Whose regular colds finally turned into pneumonia thanks to this rainy island!

BOSIE And then when her father died too, penniless, she was about as low as she could get.

SOPHIA is now completely slumped over her work under the weight of her misery, only a hand still moving in front of her on the floor on her paper.

JINDAN Come, we must rise Sophia up, for she has much to do! I have here letters from Bamba –

BOSIE And I've got a load from Catherine –

JINDAN Let us see who can get the most letters to Sophia the quickest, this side of the room you will help me –

BOSIE And this side, you're my team! Let's see if we can get her back on her feet!

The narrators run a game, giving the letters out to the back of the audience who pass them forward hand to hand until they reach the front, where two audience members appointed to be the 'posties', deliver the letters to SOPHIA, who rallies and cheers as the letters arrive.

When she is up on her feet and back to her happy self we saw in the nursery with her sisters, the game is over.

JINDAN Most marvellous work, friends! Look how Sophia is recovered! But what is she to do now? No mother, no father, all their possessions and the family home sold to cover the debts.

BOSIE Ah ha! Well, this is where good old Queen Victoria steps in and sets the sisters up at Hampton Court! Hands up if you've been? Oh, it's lovely, all moats, and mazes and gardens.

SOPHIA nips backstage to put on a longer, Edwardian white skirt to go over her current costume.

The pictures change to show Hampton Court and its surrounds. SOPHIA returns to stage with another card which says 'Hampton Court, London, 1896' and reads it.

BOSIE Now, the people allowed to live at Hampton Court were them that had given the highest service to the realm, going and fighting wars, that sort of thing.

JINDAN But of course, you often die of fighting wars, so Hampton Court was generally filled with widows, daughters and sisters. Basically, hundreds of posh, left over, white women.

BOSIE Meaning when Bamba, Catherine and Sophia moved into their new residence by the river, they stuck out a bit! The sisters soon shocked the other residents at Hampton Court.

JINDAN We need you to be people living at Hampton Court.

BOSIE Now, when those posh people were shocked, they would say, "I say, by Jove, that's a bit much!"

JINDAN So, when we point at you, that's what you say. Let's practise ...

They practise so the audience can say the line on cue.

JINDAN Very good!

BOSIE Sophia kicks off the comments by galloping her horse and walking her pack of dogs through the perfectly manicured gardens! And the residents said —

SOPHIA gallops through the audience on a hobby horse.

BOSIE points at the audience to say, 'I say, by Jove, that's a bit much!'

JINDAN Which was nothing compared to Bamba roaring around in her shocking new motorcar!

SOPHIA *(Popping head out from backstage)* Beep! Beep!

JINDAN Which made the residents say —

JINDAN dons driving goggles loudly beeps an old-fashioned car horn as she points to the audience to say — 'I say, by Jove, that's a bit much!'

BOSIE And there were also whispers that Catherine was showing signs of being in love.

BOSIE makes a heart shape with her hands.

JINDAN What on earth is wrong with young love?

BOSIE Nothing at all, but I think some people were shocked that Catherine was in love with Lina the governess and that they were both women.

JINDAN *(who is quite shocked by this)* Oh my goodness!

BOSIE It's quite normal and these days we'd say, 'good luck to 'em', but back then it of course made the residents say —

She points at the audience to say, 'I say, by Jove, that's a bit much!'

JINDAN But all this pales when compared to Sophia's adoption of the most controversial, challenging, radical contraption of her day! I'm talking of course about the bicycle!

SOPHIA *(riding around the stage or hall on her bike)* Woo hoo! Freedom!

BOSIE The residents were so outraged by hot, sweaty, freedom loving women riding all over the place –

JINDAN – especially non-white ones –

BOSIE – that they *all* said –

She and JINDAN both encourage the audience to say all together – 'I say, by Jove, that's a bit much!'

Throwing her bike to one side, very pleased with herself, SOPHIA gets cloth to drape herself in fashionably.

JINDAN Gone is that anxious little girl! This lively young woman actually courts the press.

BOSIE Her sisters worry she's taking after her dad with her extravagant spending, insisting on being dressed in the latest fashions from Paris.

SOPHIA stands like a model while BOSIE and JINDAN drape the long piece of material around her that JINDAN entered in.

BOSIE Hum, it looks like we ran out of budget for the latest fashions, isn't this the rags you were wearing at the beginning?

JINDAN I'll have you know this is the beggar disguise I used to escape from prison right under the noses of my British guards.

BOSIE *(impressed)* You never did?!

JINDAN Yes! And I left nothing but a letter saying, 'For years you put me in a cage. For all your locks and your sentries, I got out by magic! I told you not to push me too hard!'

BOSIE Larks! How did you do it?

JINDAN Do you consider yourself British?

BOSIE All my life and beyond death!

JINDAN Then I'll never tell!

BOSIE Bother.

JINDAN *(as they untangle SOPHIA from the material)* And so Sophia loved the Hampton Court home, but it was not so for her sisters. Bamba longed to live in India —

BOSIE *(As Catherine)* And Catherine, much as I loved Saff, soon found that my patience was running out as my little sister's hobbies took over the house!

While she's been talking, SOPHIA has been piling up her stuff around BOSIE — the material and dog stuff — and during BOSIE's next line she and JINDAN throw a large number of toy dogs across the stage to each other, adding them to the pile —

BOSIE *(continued as Catherine)* I especially resented the dog breeding!

SOPHIA How can you say my darling fur babies are dirty, needy and selfish? Why, they are winning awards at competitive exhibitions up and down the country! *(to one of the dogs)* Aren't you my gorgeous ikkle Joe? Yes, you are, yes you are!

JINDAN So, Catherine takes herself off to Germany with her beloved governess Lina, and Bamba eventually succeeds in her dream to move to India, to live out her days in the Sikh kingdom of her ancestors.

BOSIE And Sophia is left all to herself, all over again, in the residency in Hampton Court.

SOPHIA *(looking around sadly at the empty home she has created and is left in)* I say, by Jove, that's a bit much ...

A beat as JINDAN and BOSIE watch SOPHIA sympathetically; then BOSIE gets a suitcase. She folds up the cloth, adds other items from the stage, packing up SOPHIA for a trip.

JINDAN What are you doing?

BOSIE She can't stay here like this, moping she is! She needs to get away; I'm sending her on a trip. She can visit her sister.

JINDAN Which sister?

BOSIE Catherine?

JINDAN No, no, no. She will need to take her beloved Joe dog; Catherine hates the dogs. She must go to Bamba!

BOSIE But Bamba's in India! The British will never let her go!

JINDAN Well, they do make quite a fuss, it's a theme throughout her life, them trying to stop her going over, they keep a secret file on her –

BOSIE They never do!

JINDAN Oh yes, they keep very close tabs on the family of the Maharaja, – the spying Valati choor! *(English thief)* – but she finally convinces them she must go because Bamba is being poisoned.

BOSIE She's what?!

JINDAN Oh, she's not really, but she believes she is, and her fear, her paranoia is making her ill. Sophia must go to her! Go on, get your things!

BOSIE Me? I'm not working for her at this point, I don't even know her yet, I'm still at school! She must have had other maids.

JINDAN *(gathering the suitcase, hat boxes, pushing dog paraphernalia at BOSIE to carry)* Of course she does, I'm playing one too, she takes two on the boat! And you need to play the chap she meets onboard, too.

BOSIE I'm playing a maid then a bloke?

JINDAN Yes, and we're the noises of the dog too.

BOSIE Saints preserve us!

As her maids, JINDAN and BOSIE hustle SOPHIA's things on to the ship, while she follows, giving directions, as if they are bustling through a busy dockyard with bags and the dog, being jostled and making their way through the crowds. Before she leaves the stage to do this, SOPHIA holds up a card that says 'London Docks, a ship leaving for India, 1906'.

SOPHIA *(to her maids)* And when you find my cabin, set up Joe's basket by my bed, I'll stay with him on the deck for a while.

JINDAN/BOSIE *(as maids)* Yes miss.

JINDAN also makes the noises of Joe the Pomeranian. JINDAN manipulates the Joe dog, a toy on a wire.

SOPHIA tries to keep track of Joe who is bouncing around her feet clamouring for attention.

BOSIE has put on a man's overcoat and hat and prepares to re-enter the action as another passenger, a chap who will come to be known in SOPHIA's diaries as THE MADMAN.

SOPHIA Joe, my darling, get down, no paws on mummy's dress – and don't do that there, I told you to go before we got onboard! Joe, sweetheart, calm down and just breath in that sea air. *(Joe moves from over-enthusiastic barking to sounding like a dog about to be sick)* Err, are you sick, Joe? Stop running around like a loon then!

THE MADMAN, a fellow passenger in smart travelling clothes merrily whistling The Skye Boat Song, has crossed Joe's path at just the wrong time. His jaunty progress across deck is stopped by Joe running around and around his feet and then being sick on his shoe.

SOPHIA Oh Joe, my darling, are you alright?

THE MADMAN: This is a 'Joe', is it? This vomiting powder puff?

SOPHIA *(bridling at this description of her dog)* How dare you! Joe is an award-winning Pomeranian, a standard bearer for his breed, and a *(words fail her in her outrage)* ... wonderful boy!

THE MADMAN: Well, he's not a wonderful seafarer, is he? Or shoe-shiner.

SOPHIA Oh, your shoe ...

JINDAN/MAID: *(re-entering the action)* He's calmed down now, miss!

SOPHIA What? *(seeing the lead)* Oh, very good, just hold on to him for a little while longer –

The Maid picks up Joe gingerly. THE MADMAN goes to leave.

THE MADMAN: I say, do walk your powder puff here tomorrow, I'll wear old shoes.

He goes.

JINDAN/MAID: Who was that, miss?

SOPHIA I have absolutely no idea!

JINDAN She never did find out his name, that chap, though he entertained her everyday with his daft ramblings –

BOSIE – In her diaries she just referred to him as the Madman!

JINDAN And then, after months at sea, he never said goodbye when they docked in India, just vanished like a ghost!

BOSIE The cad! I'll never play him again!

SOPHIA I don't care! *(she does)* I'd be happy never to say another goodbye in my life! Come on Joe!

As SOPHIA stands, JINDAN goes up and holds her for a moment, as BOSIE goes to the suitcase and gets out the white material. She gives one end to JINDAN and they stretch it across the stage. As the following dialogue is spoken, we see accompanying images on the cloth.

BOSIE Sophia throws herself into exploring the markets of India with her sister Bamba, she talks to thinkers and freedom fighters, and for the first time in her life most people look like her –

On the cloth flicker images of Indian markets and political gatherings at the time of SOPHIA's visit.

JINDAN *(as market trader, in Punjabi)* Pretty miss, you hungry for lunch? Best Panipuri at my stall, aloo chaat fit for a princess!

An image of Sarla Devi flickers in and out with the British military presence on the streets of India, of soldiers with Indian women.

JINDAN Radical thinkers tell her –

BOSIE If our menfolk will not rise up and defend us from the outrages of the British soldiers, we will train each other physically and spiritually!

An image of Gopal Krishna Gokhale and Indian protests appear on the cloth.

JINDAN Freedom fighters declare –

BOSIE No taxation without representation! I shall never obey any law in the making of which I have not had a hand!

JINDAN *(as market trader, trying again in Urdu)* I am telling you, pretty lady, at my stall I feed you like the Lion of the Punjab, you understand?

SOPHIA I'm sorry, I don't understand, can you tell me in English?

JINDAN So, they do speak to her in English, oh yes! They tell her about the famines, millions dead as the British funnel money, crops and resources away from India. *(Images of the famines in India under British rule)* And when she returns to England and steps off the boat, her own eyes tell her how her countrymen are valued when they can no longer be put to work.

The cloth carries pictures of the Lascars, wretched groups of Indian men in rags huddling around the London docks.

SOPHIA walks over to the cloth holding a sign that says, 'London docks, on returning to England, 1907'.

SOPHIA These Indian farmers have been put off their land with nothing by the British who then make them work on the merchant boats leaving India, and when they arrive in London the shipping companies just leave them to starve and freeze at the docks! Gone, they're quite gone from their families, and they'll never see them again.

BOSIE So, Sophia turns her feelings, her knowledge, her experiences into action! She hits up her rich friends and builds a safe haven for the Indian shipmen that in only five years will provide urgent help to 5,000 of the stranded men.

The images on the cloth start to be intercut with flames, images of Gandhi and Gopal Krishna Gokhale, of revolt in India, of hunger striking suffragettes and horses being used against both Indians and suffragettes.

JINDAN She's a woman inflamed by her times! A fuse has been lit, in Sophia and so many around her — is might always right?

The images scrolling faster now move between campaigns against vivisection, workers' rights, endangered species.

BOSIE Should animals be eaten? Or sacrificed in the name of science? Whole species of birds made extinct in the name of fashion?

JINDAN Gandhi's imagination is set alight by women campaigning for the vote in England —

BOSIE And speaking of suffragettes ...

The lights change and the images snap off.

SOPHIA grabs a stack of placards.

BOSIE *(cont.)* They covered a lot of ground, did some joined-up thinking! Let's play Women's Rights, Then and Now!

JINDAN and BOSIE teach the audience to vote 'Then' by putting their hands on their heads and 'Now' by putting their hands on their shoulders.

SOPHIA (as actor) then shows the audience placards with slogans from suffrage campaigns for the vote, Reclaim the Night, or Indian Women's rights campaigns now.

The audience vote by placing their hands on their heads or shoulders to show if they think the slogan is 'Then' or 'Now'.

When the quote on the card is revealed by JINDAN or BOSIE to be 'then' or 'now', SOPHIA tells the audience what or where the quote is from, for example if it's a Reclaim the Night slogan or a Suffragette one, one from Victorian women English campaigners or from modern Indian women activists.

The final placard says, 'No taxation without representation'.

JINDAN Ah, this is 'Then', and one of my favourites! 'No taxation without representation'! It means a government shouldn't take people's money if those people cannot vote! It's how great revolutionaries like Basanti Devi and Mahatma Gandhi helped to free India.

BOSIE Hang about, that's one of the most famous suffrage campaigns. Why should men be allowed to be slavers, criminals or alcoholics and **not** lose the vote, while women could be mothers, key workers, teachers, even politicians and still not *have* it?!

SOPHIA flips around her placard revealing another timeline card on the back saying 'Sophia at a suffragette meeting, 1910'

SOPHIA *(as if explaining her presence at the meeting)* You see I recognised the idea from my time in India, when I saw your fliers, just brilliant! So, I went along to hear your daughter speak, Mrs Pankhurst —

JINDAN and BOSIE jump and quickly gear up for the scene. They both make a grab for the biggest hat —

BOSIE I want to be Emmeline Pankhurst, the leader of the Suffragette movement!

JINDAN You can be her helper, Annie Kenney!

BOSIE Just 'cos she's working class; you want to be all the posh people!

JINDAN I was the maid last time!

This is true, so BOSIE gives up the hat with a 'humph' and picks up a smaller, less obviously posh one.

BOSIE Annie Kenney, and her a northerner, whatever next!

For the rest of this scene BOSIE plays ANNIE KENNEY, a kind, practical, Mancunian suffragette in her later middle age and JINDAN plays Emmeline Pankhurst, the matriarch of the Women's Social and Political Union (WSPU).

*At points in the scene, **BOSIE** and **JINDAN** enlist the students around them to be other members of the meeting.*

SOPHIA So, I went along to hear your daughter speak, Mrs Pankhurst, and I just knew I was for your movement, heart and soul!

JINDAN *as* **EMMELINE** *(with the hat triumphantly clamped to her head)* – And which of my daughters so inspired you, your **Highness**?

SOPHIA It was Christabel, Mrs Pankhurst –

EMMELINE Please, call me Emmeline. Well Annie, what it could mean for us! The support of a **Princess**, eh? What do you say, shall we vote her in?

They lead the vote, responding to and riffing on whatever the students vote around them but not for long and pressing forward to vote her in.

ANNIE It's an aye from me!

SOPHIA And I will support in any way I'm able, if you can find use for me.

EMMELINE We can and will! We'd be mad not to, imagine the papers when **Queen Victoria's Goddaughter** is the key speaker at our next rally!

SOPHIA *(we suddenly see the little girl from the start of the play)* Oh, please –

EMMELINE Just think of what they will write when high society's most fashionable **Princess** tells the crowds 'Deeds not Words!' outside of parliament!

SOPHIA Goodness, please, no!

Both women stare at her in surprise. A beat.

ANNIE I'm so sorry, Highness, but when you said you wanted to help –

SOPHIA And I do!

EMMELINE But perhaps you don't want to be in the papers?

SOPHIA *(thinking it through)* No, I don't believe that should bother me, or at least it should not stop me doing what I thought was right.

EMMELINE You're frightened of crowds then?

SOPHIA Not at all, it's speaking ...

ANNIE Speaking, Highness?

SOPHIA To speak before people, in public, I never thought of it but now I do I just know I should hate it!

ANNIE Oh, but I felt that at first, but now I speak at meetings like these all over the country!

SOPHIA *(shuddering at the thought)* You're very brave, the thought, it makes me feel I might actually be sick. Is there really nothing else you can do with me?

The two suffragettes look at each other. A beat.

EMMELINE Why my dear, there is so much more we can do with you, that is, that you can do, if you are absolutely sure we can't persuade you to speak in public —

SOPHIA makes an involuntary dry gag.

ANNIE Motion to the meeting to stop asking the Princess about public speaking before she is actually sick!

The vote is taken about whether to pass this motion, jokes can be made about those that want to see her be sick, but ultimately the vote is moved on.

EMMELINE Don't give it another thought ... if you're not adverse to publicity —

SOPHIA — Absolutely love it!

EMMELINE – We'll get you selling our paper! I can see the front pages now, **'Princess Singh** sells *The Suffragette* outside Hampton Court'!

ANNIE And of course we need famous women to withhold their taxes, but they fine you, and if you don't pay it's a prison sentence.

SOPHIA I am quite prepared to withhold my taxes, not pay fines and run that risk. In fact, I'd be honoured.

JINDAN and BOSIE pick up the white cloth, wrapping it around SOPHIA and holding it at the back of her so she is walking into it, and it supports her as she leans forward, her placard held aloft.

BOSIE And it was Sophia's honour, her mind, her heart, that kept her in the crowd of suffragettes outside parliament later that same year on a day that would go down in history as Black Friday.

Images start to appear on the cloth of the crowds and police massing on Black Friday.

BOSIE *(cont.)*: Knowing that a large gathering of suffragettes was coming to parliament, the Home Secretary, a young Winston Churchill, instructed the police not to make any proper arrests but instead stop the women from getting to the gates of Westminster at all costs.

JINDAN He invited the police to use any physical force required to repress the women, telling them to hit the women's breasts as he hoped it might give them cancer.

The images on the cloth start to show the violence of the police to the suffragettes.

BOSIE *(shocked)* Winston Churchill actually ordered that?

JINDAN Those were his express commands. And how imaginative the police proved themselves to be in following their instructions. They tossed women between them like dolls, throwing them repeatedly to the ground to exhaust them.

BOSIE Some swung their helmets like clubs, some hurled women into the paths of on-coming vehicles.

JINDAN To humiliate as well as wound, the police grabbed the women's bodies, ripped their clothes and pulled up their skirts, telling the men in the crowd to join them in teaching these females their place.

BOSIE To my shame as an Englishwoman, some men joined in, but other on lookers were appalled and tried to pull women to safety.

Now SOPHIA is pulling and moving against the material as she struggles to get through a thick, moving crowd pushing her from all sides.

SOPHIA You, officer, you take your hands off her! Can't you see she's nearly unconscious? What is your identification number?

JINDAN And Sophia is in the midst of all this. For hours she is trapped helpless watching the violence, until she manages to slip through the police barrier. Then she pushes through the thick of the assaults, trying to aid women who are standing up again and again after being slapped, beaten and kicked to the ground.

SOPHIA Come back here, Constable V700! This is an abomination!

BOSIE She don't get arrested though! Not Queen Victoria's goddaughter! Try as she might, not one stretch.

SOPHIA tidies herself after the crowd, dresses herself smartly.

JINDAN Yes, she wasn't lying to herself about that, she is more than willing to do her stint in Holloway to advance the cause of women's rights.

SOPHIA is collecting things she needs from the stage, including a rolled-up banner.

BOSIE Gets very inventive she does! She refuses to give her details to the census, telling the authorities –

SOPHIA – If women don't count, neither shall they be counted!

JINDAN She goes to the highest levels writing to Churchill himself to –

SOPHIA Hold Constable V700 accountable for his disgraceful violence!

JINDAN – To no avail of course but it all adds to the government's spy file on her, the Valati choor!

BOSIE And over and over the suffragettes ask her to speak to them, for them, at rallies, at meetings, and always she replies –

SOPHIA *(writing a letter responding to the request)* I will come to the meeting with pleasure, but I do hope you have found someone else to *(with another dry gag at the thought)* speak. I *very much* prefer not to, and I shall only say about five words!

JINDAN And still, she does not see the inside of a prison cell, even when her most outrageous performances take her all the way to Number 10!

BOSIE Picture the scene! 1911 and the old monarch has died; a new King has been crowned –

SOPHIA, dressed beautifully, enters humming & singing under her breath snatches of Laurence Housman's, 'Woman This and Woman That' published January 1910 and usually performed by Decima Moore, one of the founders of the Actresses' Franchise League. Lines can be heard through the following narration as SOPHIA fortifies herself with the song, keeping her spirits up, building up her nerve.

BOSIE It's a chilly February morning, and the streets of Whitehall are packed with finely dressed ladies and gents, all waiting to see Prime Minister Asquith –

JINDAN Who has long refused to receive the suffragettes' petitions or listen to their demands –

BOSIE Listening instead to the new King's first Speech before Parliament.

SOPHIA *(singing):* 'Get out!' the politicians cried; 'we want no women here!'

JINDAN *(throwing BOSIE a policeman's hat):* Of course, there are a lot of policemen –

BOSIE I said I wouldn't play a bloke again!

JINDAN It's not the same one from the boat.

BOSIE I bet this one isn't any nicer!

JINDAN He is at first, because he thinks Sophia is just another upper-class lady waiting to cheer the PM's car.

SOPHIA *(singing):* "M.P.s behind the railings stood and laughed to see the fun.

And bold policemen knocked us down, because we would not run."

BOSIE/POLICEMAN Morning mam, did you call for a policeman?

SOPHIA Oh, no, I was just saying, so many here to see the fun!

POLICEMAN Yes mam, there's many as want to see the two most powerful men in the Empire mark the beginning of a new era – a fine, historic day indeed!

SOPHIA Will Asquith walk to Parliament do you think?

POLICEMAN He'll take his car mam, though it's only down the road, you can almost see Big Ben from here. But we can't take no chances, you never know what hooligan, nutter or suffragette might try and mob 'im.

SOPHIA How dreadful.

POLICEMAN But don't you worry, as soon as that door opens, you'll get a look at the PM, as he makes his way to his car.

JINDAN The crowds swelled as the morning wore on, and Sophia kept her hat low over her eyes in case anyone more astute than this plod –

BOSIE Oi!

JINDAN – recognised her as the rebel princess and blew her cover!

SOPHIA *(singing, almost chanting the words to herself to psych herself up)* "We went before a magistrate, who would not hear us speak;

To a drunken brute who beat his wife he only gave a week;"

JINDAN *(putting on a smart hat and making her way into the audience)*: And suddenly there he was, the Prime Minister...

BOSIE I knew you'd end up being the PM!

JINDAN ...making his way out of number 10 and past the crowds right towards her!

JINDAN as ASQUITH makes her way towards the front row as if they are the crowds waiting to greet and cheer the PM.

SOPHIA *(singing):* "But we were sent to Holloway a calendar month or more

Because we dared, against his will, to knock at Asquith's door."

With this she throws herself forward at ASQUITH who has just turned away from the front row to wave to the crowds further away and perhaps say a few words –

JINDAN/ASQUITH Ladies and gentlemen, thank you for your support on this auspicious day –

SOPHIA drowns out his words with her song, this next verse happening while she takes a concealed banner from her person (a muff if possible) saying "Votes for Women" and fights to drape it over ASQUITH (or his car, depending how this is staged) while the POLICEMAN tries to catch up with her and stop her –

SOPHIA *(singing):* "For it's woman this, and woman that, and 'Woman, say your say!'

But it's 'What's the woman up to?' when she tries to show the way;

When she tries to show the way, my friends, she tries to show the way –

And the woman means to show it – that is why she's out today"

Finally subdued by the POLICEMAN, SOPHIA is borne away from ASQUITH who becomes JINDAN again.

POLICEMAN *(bundling SOPHIA away)*: Well, you played me for a right Charlie there! It comes to something when you can't even trust the posh ones!

SOPHIA *(sighing, breathless, but triumphant)*: "Well, it's woman this and woman that!"

POLICEMAN Oh, get along you!

SOPHIA Aren't you arresting me?

POLICEMAN Not on your nelly, your majesty!

JINDAN Sophia may have failed to get arrested, but she certainly made the papers! The next day the headlines ran "Princess as Picket!"

SOPHIA gets out the scribbled notes from earlier in her chaotic handwriting, as if creating and trying to order a speech.

She holds up and reads out a sign that says, 'Sophia in court, 1911'.

BOSIE Sophia finally sees the inside of a court though, and it's not for her militant suffrage or her direct actions –

JINDAN No, my friends, then as now, it's all about the money!

SOPHIA *or* **BOSIE** *or all 3 of the cast (singing)*:

"For it's woman this, and woman that, and 'Woman, go away!'
But it's 'Share and share alike, ma'am!' when the taxes are to pay!
When taxes are to pay, my friends, the taxes are to pay
Oh, it's 'Please to pay up promptly!' when the taxes are to pay!"

JINDAN sees it first and makes her way over to the judge's wig.

JINDAN By hook or by crook I will judge by the book!

BOSIE *(grabbing it before JINDAN)* By eggs and by bacon I'm sure you're mistaken! Not after you managed to wrangle playing the blinkin' PM! *(Placing the wig firmly on her head and taking position stage left)* I'm the judge, you can be Castello, Sophia's lawyer.

JINDAN grudgingly takes her position in the court as CASTELLO and BOSIE continues as the JUDGE, having a lot of fun with a gross, spitty stereotype of a judge.

JUDGE I see Her Highness has sent her representation once more to answer for the numerous charges against her *(consults his paperwork)*, let me see, what are they this time? She has refused to pay her taxes, again; she has employed a groom, dogs and a carriage without the necessary licences; Dear, dear, no wonder she doesn't want to give first-hand account of her quite unaccountable actions!

CASTELLO Actually, your honour, my client her Highness Princess Sophia Alexandrovna Jindan Duleep Singh will be answering the charges herself today. *(aside to his client, looking at her doubtfully)* Do you think you will be able to, Highness?

SOPHIA *(rustling her papers, reordering them)* Yes, yes, I feel quite *(dry gag)* ... what I mean is that I shall be doing it so there it is! *(she has said this last statement as much to herself as to him)*

JUDGE *(surprised she is there to speak)* Well, is that so? Then, your Highness, the court shall hear you!

SOPHIA *(her hands tremble on the notes, but when she speaks her voice is steady)* I am unable conscientiously to pay money to the state, as I am not allowed to exercise any control over its expenditure, neither am I allowed any voice in the choosing of members of Parliament, whose salaries I have to help to pay. This is very unjustified. When the women of England are enfranchised and the State acknowledge me as a citizen, I shall, of course, pay my share willingly towards its upkeep. If I am not a fit person for the purposes of representation, why should I be a fit person for taxation?

BOSIE *(proudly, ditching the wig)* That made it into *The Times*, that did!

SOPHIA fans herself with her papers with relief.

JINDAN But soon there is other news, news of a war the like of which the world has never seen, a great and terrible war that will leave lives up turned across the globe. A war that changes the course of the suffragette movement to which Sophia has given her life.

SOPHIA holds up a card and reads: '1914 – World War One'.

BOSIE They don't agree, you see, the suffragettes, even amongst themselves, about World War One. You see some say all campaigning for the vote must stop so the country can pull together for victory against Germany. But many say this war is just the rich land-grabbing from each other and using the blood of the working classes to mark their territories.

JINDAN And what does this mean for Indians under British rule? It means they are of course drafted in their thousands, without proper uniforms or boots, from the warmth of Mother India to the freezing, drenched trenches of Europe. So appalling are the conditions, so many the losses, that one Indian boy writes to his family, 'this is not war, it is the ending of the world; my comrades go to their deaths like corn being ground in a mill.'

BOSIE So now Sophia has a new cause.

BOSIE and JINDAN re-order the stage, making a hospital wing. When it is ready JINDAN puts on a dressing gown and puts herself into a hospital bed while SOPHIA shows a sign which says, 'Soldiers hospital, Brighton, 1916' (she can always read these out while showing if needed)

BOSIE *(cont.)* Towns like Brighton are being flooded with wounded Indian soldiers and Sophia joins the Red Cross to help nurse them. *(putting on a white pinny and nurses' hat)* Here she is now arriving for her first shift, meeting her fellow volunteer nurses –

JINDAN Who you are going to play!

BOSIE I was just about to say that!

JINDAN You will play one of the patients –

BOSIE I'm not playing a bloke again! You do it this time!

JINDAN Use your eyes, I'm already doing it! We will both play male patients in this scene, Indian men who are injured from the Battle of the Somme, but first you are the nurse.

BOSIE I know! *(Adopts posh voice and the clipped, no-nonsense manner of a military wife of long standing and, taking SOPHIA by the arm, propels her towards the 'beds' but weaving up and down the aisles as if they are going up and down long, thin corridors)* Ah, your Highness, I'm Sister Powell-Sinclair, I can't tell you how honoured we are to have you here. These poor little sepoys are arriving in droves from the front, and in such a state. How do you want them to address you? As your Highness? Or are you incognito as it were?

SOPHIA Incognito I should think, I'm here as a woman and a nurse, not a princess.

SISTER: Marvellous! And of course, it picks the men up no end just to have us talk to them in Hindustani!

SOPHIA Oh, I can't speak it.

SISTER I'm sorry, Punjabi will be just as meaningful to them.

SOPHIA I only speak English.

SISTER Well, I never! Do excuse me, it never occurred to me that an Indian Princess wouldn't be able to speak her own language, but then I suppose why should you, you've never lived there!

SOPHIA No, I've visited, but I live here, I'm British, so English is my own language. Do you speak to them in Hindustani?

SISTER Oh yes, my Nathaniel was stationed in Delhi. Shall we?

She ushers SOPHIA into the 'ward'. JINDAN as a wounded soldier is in her 'bed' struggling with the composition of a letter and SOPHIA and the SISTER act as if there are men in all the other 'beds'.

SISTER *(cont.)* As you can see this is the mid-afternoon lull, the men have had lunch and their medication and are mostly resting. *(seeing JINDAN as EKAM is awake)* Not taking your nap, Ekam?

EKAM My daughter, she wants me to teach her English, she's smart, she wants to go to university, but I struggle with writing the words to her she wants.

SISTER Our new nurse, Nurse Singh here, can help with that.

SOPHIA Of course, I'd be happy to help if I can.

As the SISTER hurries off, SOPHIA sits by EKAM. BOSIE takes off her pinny and nurse's hat, puts on a dressing gown and takes her place in one of the nearby 'beds' as another resting man.

EKAM Forgive me, it is, I am *(he struggles for the English words, he wants to tell her he is confused by her looks, yet her not speaking his language)*, you not from India?

SOPHIA *(shaking her head)* I'm British.

EKAM *(staring at her)* This very strange!

SOPHIA What is it you want to say to your daughter?

EKAM I want to say I get better, I come home, I bring her books. She not fear for me, so far from home.

SOPHIA Should I write it out for you in English?

EKAM Oh, please, thank you!

SOPHIA *(taking paper and pen from EKAM)* I am so sorry for your daughter. My sister Catherine lives in Germany and can't get permission to come back. And of course, now she is seen as an enemy there, we're frantic with worry.

EKAM Your sister, she marry Germany?

SOPHIA She lives with her German friend, an intimate friend.

BOSIE as GUNEET the soldier has woken up and looks around.

GUNEET *(in Punjabi)* On these wards, never a moment's peace, a man might as well be back at the Somme. (Ek mend shanti neh. Banda mu Somme paunch kia)

SOPHIA I'm so sorry, did we wake you?

EKAM *(in Punjabi)* Look, Nurse Singh, she's pretty! She's new!

GUNEET *(in Punjabi, staring at SOPHIA)* Do you not know to whom you speak, Ekam, you fool? This is the Granddaughter of the Lion of the Punjab! (Tu pa shan diney. Dek neh suk ta, o shah di Punjab po tia)

EKAM *(in English, to SOPHIA)* Guneet says you Granddaughter of the Lion of the Punjab, is he mad?

GUNEET *(in Punjabi)* Look! It's Princess Sophia Singh! [Dek! Raj kumari Sofia Singh a!]

SOPHIA Do you know me?

EKAM Guneet is right, I see you, many years ago in India, you sit by Lala Lajpat Rai on stage and he says, 'India grows the cotton, India make the cloth, Indians should keep the money!' You are our Princess!

Like his friend, he is astonished and tearful.

SOPHIA What a memory you have, to care for us, I don't know why you should after all this time.

EKAM You are our Princess, from our empire!

GUNEET *(in Punjabi, with pride and triumph)* Bole Son Nihal!

EKAM I can tell you response —

SOPHIA No, I think I know it, people shouted that out to us in India, it's a Sikh cry of triumph, isn't it? Oh, can I recall it? Sat Sri Akal! *(which means 'God is the ultimate truth')*

Both men are elated at her use of the language.

EKAM *and* **GUNEET** Bole Son Nihal!

SOPHIA Sat Sri Akal!

EKAM *and* **GUNEET** Bole Son Nihal!

SOPHIA Sat Sri Akal!

The men bow their heads humbly, and they are both weeping.

SOPHIA gets up and begins collecting her belongings from around the stage and arranging them centre-stage – a slow, considered process that happens throughout the last part of the play. As part of this she gets out a sign that says 'Sophia's home in Buckinghamshire, 1940 onwards ...'

SOPHIA The cards feel heavier now, I think it's because I'm older, look *(pointing at the date on the card)* 1940s, the last card was in 1916, I was 24 years younger!

BOSIE Of course, the best years of Sophia's life are about to start after this –

JINDAN My friend, really? In her later years, Sophia often faced her cruellest foe, the depression and sadness that made her tetchy with her servants, reclusive from her friends.

BOSIE Ah ha, that's as maybe but it's in this part of her life that I come and work for her! And I wasn't frightened of her moods. I'd just say, 'Princess, you stop your pouting!' and in no time she'd be herself again. And she took me to India!

JINDAN She had to because when you found out she was going you cried and cried and wouldn't come out of the bathroom till she went and bought you a ticket she could ill afford!

BOSIE Well, I wanted to see an elephant that bad! And we got you back there, that was important to her.

JINDAN Yes, she took my ashes back to Lahore, back to my husband's shrine, and I found peace after my long exile.

BOSIE And she became godmother to my little girl when I married –

JINDAN I can't believe you asked her to do that!

BOSIE My princess was delighted to be asked, oh she was scared to hold the baby, but she'd sing to her –

SOPHIA *(Singing)* Somewhere over the rainbow, way up high.

JINDAN Oh, that heart, that burned and beat and held, for dear life, for a better life for others. And that is tired now, that has earned some rest.

BOSIE And when my little girl got older, she'd go walking with her, and she'd tell her all about the world and elections and how important they were.

SOPHIA (*addressing the audience.*) Now, I want a solemn promise from you; you are never, ever not to vote! You must promise me. When you are allowed to vote you are never, ever to fail to do so. You don't realise how far we've come. Promise me.

She stands behind her belongings and pulls a sheet up from the floor to represent getting into bed. She sighs, she is tired, she pulls the covers up to her chin, curling up. BOSIE stands by her head and strokes it.

JINDAN stands on the other side of the bed. The bed has things from SOPHIA's life gathered around it, the suitcases, dog, suffragette sash, nurses' hat & bag.

Images flicker across the white bed and the figure in it, going back through the play from the start, marking the episodes of SOPHIA's life.

JINDAN *goes to cover her over with the white cloth.*

BOSIE No! Don't cover her up.

JINDAN We have to let her go, Bosie, she's tired.

BOSIE But I don't want her to be dead!

JINDAN Everyone in the play is dead, remember?

BOSIE But we still have so much to tell them!

JINDAN I know, we haven't talked about the young evacuees she took in and adored in World War Two.

BOSIE Or her support of Indian freedom fighters.

JINDAN Or how she didn't stop when women finally got the vote in Britain but campaigned to get them the vote in India!

BOSIE Or how she described her life's purpose as

BOSIE & JINDAN "The advancement of women!"

JINDAN And we haven't told my favourite story about what a thorn she was in the side of King George V. He cried out to his ministers,

BOSIE "Have we no hold on her?!"

JINDAN But we have less than an hour to talk about our princess.

BOSIE You can't fit a whole life into that time!

JINDAN The play must end, Bosie.

BOSIE But if it ends, we won't exist once the students leave the room!

SOPHIA Sophia and Jindan and Bosie won't exist anymore, but maybe the students will talk about them, and tell other people about Sophia's story.

SOPHIA holds up and reads the last card which says, 'Princess Sophia died in her sleep in 1948, age 71 and, at her instructions, her ashes were taken to India for burial'. She resumes her position, ready to die.

JINDAN & BOSIE lift the white cloth to cover SOPHIA.

After final projection, sheet drops and all three actors take a bow.

The End.

More great plays from Aurora Metro Books

ADA by Emily Holyoake
ISBN 978-1-912430-09-3   £9.99

THREE WOMEN by Matilda Velevitch
ISBN 978-1-912430-35-2   £9.99

NOOR by Azma Dar
ISBN 978-1-912430-72-7   £9.99

COMBUSTION by Asif Khan
ISBN 978-1-911501-91-6   £9.99

DIARY OF A HOUNSLOW GIRL by Ambreen Razia
ISBN 978-0-9536757-9-1   £8.99

SPLIT/MIXED by Ery Nzaramba
ISBN 978-1-911501-97-8   £10.99

A GIRL WITH A BOOK by Nick Wood
ISBN 978-1-910798-61-4   £12.99

THE TROUBLE WITH ASIAN MEN by Sudha Bhuchar, Kristine Landon-Smith and Louise Wallinger
ISBN 978-1-906582-41-8   £8.99

WOMEN OF ASIA by Asa Palomera
ISBN 978-1-906582-94-4   £7.99

HARVEST by Manjula Padmanabhan
ISBN 978-0-9536757-7-7   £6.99

I HAVE BEFORE ME A REMARKABLE DOCUMENT by Sonja Linden
ISBN 978-0-9546912-3-3   £7.99

NEW SOUTH AFRICAN PLAYS ed. Charles J. Fourie
ISBN 978-0-9542330-1-3   £11.99

BLACK AND ASIAN PLAYS Anthology introduced by Afia Nkrumah
ISBN 978-0-9536757-4-6   £12.99

SOUTHEAST ASIAN PLAYS ed. Cheryl Robson and Aubrey Mellor
ISBN 978-1-906582-86-9   £16.99

SIX PLAYS BY BLACK AND ASIAN WOMEN WRITERS ed. Kadija George
ISBN 978-0-9515877-2-0   £12.99

www.aurorametro.com